Contents

Copyright

Disclaimers

thereof to the user. With respect to information regarding financial performance, nothing in this book should be interpreted as a statement or implication that past results are an indication of future performance. Any financial information should be talked about with a certified financial advisor before taking action upon.

Past performance does not guarantee future returns. The views expressed herein do not constitute research, investment advice or trade recommendations

Reviewing This Book

On Amazon, reviews are incredibly valuable to self-published authors. Each review helps inform other readers about the book and (hopefully) provides support to authors with positive reviews.

If you find useful information from this book, it would mean an incredible deal to me if you left a review for it on Amazon. Each review helps my books rank better on search results and helps me write better after hearing your feedback.

Goal of this book

So much of personal finance advice is focused on budgeting and saving up for retirement, but so little of the information out there covers how to optimize what to do with those savings. There's so many tips and tricks that aren't commonly known to invest, manage, and access retirement money.

In this book, I focus on the techniques and accounts that can be used to invest even more money, optimize the returns and risks while it is invested, and be able to access the money well before retirement age without breaking laws or losing a significant portion of the money to fees and penalties.

If you are wondering how enough money can be saved that the techniques and accounts in this book would even be needed, read my first book, Buy Back Your Freedom, where you can learn about the key steps you can take to have even more money to invest and reach your financial independence goals sooner.

Philosophy of Financial Independence

Retiring at 65 sucks. You have enough money and plenty of time, but no energy! You need a nap after doing the errands for the day. Every task that is a challenge now will be impossible in your twilight years. So why wait to accomplish your dreams? There are many reasons, but most people wait until they are 65 to retire simply because that's when everyone is taught you can retire. It's the way our parents, grandparents, neighbors, and coworkers do it. It's hard to make a choice when you don't know the alternatives.

There are really a huge number of options when it comes to career and retirement. The most well-known is the conventional 40 year grind at a corporate job and eventual condo in Florida, but there are other options like starting a lifestyle business that fits around your priorities, traveling around the world and only working when needed, or saving up a large amount of money for a few short years and quitting when there's enough to live off the interest.

This last option might sound like the traditional path of working until 65 but that's because people don't realize that the actual amount necessary to live off of is around $400,000 to $1,000,000 for the average individual, not the $2-$6 million dollars often given as the ideal retirement nest egg. This extreme amount actually comes from brokers and money managers encouraging clients to invest more, and padding their pockets with fees earned from the management of the money. Coupled with the fact that the typical American lifestyle is fairly lavish and luxurious, with large homes and high end cars, this enormous amount of money is necessary to maintain this lifestyle for 20 or more years in retirement.

This huge nest egg requires decades of saving and stressful, unfulfilling work to reach. When it comes down to it, we should ask ourselves "Is all this energy and time spent working and saving up worth the outcome?" Two decades of shuffleboard, bingo, brunches, and a cushy assisted living complex? It hardly seems worth the stress, overtime, and broken relationships many people deal with in order to climb the corporate ladder and get a bigger paycheck.

If you're like me and value your time and the pursuit of passions, the answer to this question is a resounding "No!" The purpose of work should be to give us enough of a challenge to engage our minds, enough money to provide for our needs, and enough free time to enjoy life, while not draining our happiness, energy, and time. For most people, their job results only in the latter.

The goal of this book is to act as a practical guide for super charging your savings, and reaching financial independence and freedom significantly earlier than 65. It is a long road that, although challenging to start, becomes easier with every step. Everyone has different life goals, obstacles, and benefits, making the advice and information in this book a starting point to develop and learn from, rather than absolute rules to follow.

Mindset of Financial Independence

Before we begin learning about the steps to reach financial independence, it's important to understand some key concepts that clarify and guide our decisions towards becoming FI (Financially Independent). From all the interviews, research, and study I have done with people who have chosen to pursue financial independence, the biggest indicator of how successful they are is their mindset on life decisions. A majority of them approach spending holistically, thinking about the consequences, alternatives, and the value that major purchases will bring. They have a strong vision for what their ideal life should look like, and are willing to take action to change their current situation to reach that ideal life. Many of them are results oriented and are willing to be the outliers who bring their lunch to work, ride public transportation, or forego the latest model of luxury car that their colleagues have just upgraded to.

Ultimately, our time is limited

A popular term in the FI community is F.I.R.E, an acronym meaning "Financially Independent, Retired Early". It might seem like financial independence and retiring early are the same thing, but there is a fairly big distinction. While retiring brings up images of mimosas on the beach, long afternoon golf games, and moving to Florida; becoming independent creates imagines of going sky diving, pursuing your passions, and crossing off items from a bucket list.

A fact of life is that we all have a limited amount of time on earth. Some are fortunate enough to have more, some unfortunately have less. Regardless, all of us must decide how we spend this finite resource. Where we allocate our limited time shows what we care about most, whether it's a job, family and friends, passions, or even possessions. We make sacrifices pursuing some goals by giving up time, money, or the opportunity to pursue other goals.

There are many different goals and passions that people pursue but, ultimately, we all want to be happy. Ideally, if we looked at where we spent our time, and compared that with what our goals and passions are, they should match up. A majority of the time, this usually isn't the case. Throughout our lives, we get tastes and glimpses of what would make us happy, but instead of pursuing it with our hearts, minds, and souls, we put it off until it is safe to pursue, which is usually after a lengthy time doing things we **aren't** passionate about, or even happy doing. We convince ourselves that what we truly want has to be put off for decades. Too often, we realize there's little time remaining to pursue what makes us happy; and we've waited on our dreams for too long and missed out on the joy that could have come from pursuing them earlier.

Ask yourself what would be the one thing that you want to do in life, regardless of how much money you would make doing it. Chances are you aren't pursuing it with all of your time and effort or even at all. Financial independence gives us the ability to pursue these passions wholeheartedly. After becoming financially independent, **You** are in complete control of what you can do, and you are not spending a third of your life at a job that drains you of energy and happiness.

Trading Your Life for Money

We spend decades working at jobs that don't fulfill us for bosses that don't have our best interests in mind, in order to earn as much money as possible. We spend this money as fast as we can during the few hours of free time we have, trying to escape stress and find the next thing that will make us happy. This may seem like a ridiculous scenario, and it is! Americans are notorious for owning fast cars, big houses, and lots of expensive gadgets. We also have the mounds of debt, stress, and unhappiness that come with all these possessions. While we've convinced ourselves that happiness comes from making and owning MORE, we don't realize it also means more stress, broken relationships, and unhappiness; however, we gladly accept this craziness as normal, and continue to trade our time for money to buy more stuff. It's very important to realize we give up memories, life changing experiences, and new friends when we decide to take the "safe" route of working a steady job until 65 and pursuing material wealth.

Salaries are great, but Wealth is even better; Wealth is freedom. But not the kind "wealth" of having a jet, a 20 bedroom mansion, and the latest model luxury car. Wealth means your money works for you instead of the other way around. A salary is like the jealous girlfriend who, when she's not getting enough attention, leaves you. Wealth is the rock steady wife that supports and cares for you, even at the low points in life. Having a steady salary is considered safe, though in reality, everyone's salary is at risk of being taken away at a moment's notice, either at the whim of cut backs due to a poor economy, or because the boss decides you haven't been improving since the last performance review. What a job really comes down to is earning money so that you can take expensive vacations and buy nice things to reward yourself for coping with the stress of your job, all during the limited free time you're left with. This means that your salary is tied directly to exchanging your time and energy for a paycheck.

True wealth leads to having complete discretion over how you spend your time. This is very contrary to how successful and wealthy people are traditionally portrayed. The first images that often come to mind when picturing wealth are a new sports car, a large house, a beach vacation home, and expensive candle lit dinners with champagne and caviar. Now if you imagine someone who spends their time at home, pursuing their hobbies with family, and developing themselves, unemployment is probably the first thing people think of. Most likely, the person who is living it up with all their luxuries is also up to their eyeballs in credit card debt and loan payments, while the person at home probably has a million dollars invested that is making even more money for them.

If we want to be "traditionally successful", we're going to need to spend a majority of our time advancing our careers, getting raises, and getting into more debt to live the lifestyle everyone expects successful people to lead, with a minority of time going to actually enjoying it. Becoming financially independent breaks this equation down and turns it from more time equals more money to just enough money equals all the time in the world. Financial independence disconnects your time from money; where after saving just enough, your time is freed and earning more money becomes a small or nonexistent part of life.

Overview of Common Accounts

There are a handful of accounts that can be used as part of everyone's journey to FI, but there often isn't a good understanding of how to use them to their full potential. This section is meant to give a basic overview of the most widespread accounts along with their strengths and weaknesses.

401k

The 401k is the most common employer benefit offered in America, while also being one of the least utilized tools with a huge potential for reducing taxes and maximizing the amount money that can be invested. It's my favorite tool to pursue financial independence because it's so simple but so powerful, yet it is unfortunately ignored by practically the whole work force.

The power of the 401k comes from its high pre-tax contributions and a huge reduction in taxable income, meaning the government takes a smaller chunk of your money. In 2016, individuals can put up to $18,000 of their pre-tax pay into an employer 401(k), and these contributions reduce the amount of income that can be taxed. If you earn $50,000 and contributed the max to a 401(k), the IRS will only tax $32,000 of it. At the 25% tax rate, this is a savings of $4,500 on taxes! Once past age 50, an additional $6,000 in contributions can be made. The one catch is that the money in the account can't be touched until you reach 59 ½ years old, but we'll see how to work around this later on.

The cherry on top of this great tax avoidance strategy is that most employers also match contributions up to a limit that changes from business to business, but the average is 3%. This match doesn't count against the limit individuals can contribute in a year, so if an employer gave a $540 match, and $18,000 was contributed, the total invested amount would be $18,540, instead of being capped at $18,000.

To show how big the savings on taxes are, let's compare two investors, both of which earn $50,000. In the first situation, our smart investor maxes out his 401(k) and gets the employer match, whereas in the second situation our oblivious investor doesn't take any advantage of his 401(k) and puts $18,000 of after tax dollars in a taxable account. After the IRS takes their portion, the smart investor will have around $42,000 in total investable money. Because the oblivious investor had to pay income taxes before investing his money, he will only have $37,500 to invest. This is nearly a $5,000 difference, just by investing the same amount of money in a tax advantaged account! Because contributions are sheltered from taxes when they are invested, the money that would have gone to taxes can also grow and benefit from compound interest.

Eventually, taxes will have to be paid at the regular income tax rate on any money taken out, whether it came from contributions, dividends, or capital gains. Since most people who are on the path to FIRE expect to have a lower yearly income in the future, and will be in a lower tax bracket, this isn't that terrible of a trade-off. Compared to paying taxes on income, investing after tax money, and paying capital gains taxes on withdrawals, this pre-tax investing advantage is huge.

Another catch is the severe penalty on withdrawals of pre-tax 401(k) contributions while you are still employed at the 401(k)'s company and also under 59 ½ years old. If you try to withdraw any money, an **excise tax** of ten percent will need to be paid on the amount distributed on top of ordinary income taxes. If you leave a company, there is the option to rollover funds into another 401(k) plan or a Traditional IRA, with a Traditional IRA being preferred because of the wider selection of investments to pick from.

Traditional IRA

The Traditional IRA is similar to a 401(k) because it essentially uses pre-tax money to invest for retirement, but compared to a 401(k), a Traditional IRA has a huge number of funds to pick from. IRA accounts are set up through brokers like Vanguard or Fidelity, and offer all of the funds available on the market, instead of the limited selection of a 401(k). Investors can use after tax money to buy funds in the account, but the IRS lets this money reduce taxable income up to the 2016 IRS limit of $5,500, turning contributions into tax reductions. After age 50, the contribution limit rises to $6,500 for 2016. This money will be taxed as normal income when withdrawn. There are steep penalties when money is withdrawn before age 59 ½, with a 10% penalty on top of income taxes. The IRS will waive this penalty with some exceptions, including a first time home purchase (up to $10,000), higher education expenses, death, disability, un-reimbursed medical expenses, or health insurance, all of which must meet certain stipulations. Money in a Traditional IRA can be rolled over into a Roth IRA, which is an important feature for a Roth Conversion Ladder, which we'll talk about in a later chapter.

The Traditional IRA can be used at any income level, unlike the Roth IRA, which has income limits. There are limits and conditions to how much can be deducted from taxable income based on income level. One of these conditions is whether you have an employer sponsored retirement account, such as a 401(k). If you are covered, there are diminishing amounts that can be deducted as income rises. If employees aren't covered by an employer plan, then all contributions can be deducted no matter how high income rises. The IRS uses Modified AGI, or modified adjusted gross income, to determine deduction eligibility and amounts. The calculation for this can be complex for some investors, but most people will just have to subtract their 401(k) contributions from their income to get their MAGI.

This is the IRS' table for 2016 deductible amounts for investors who have a retirement plan at work:

If Your Filing Status Is...	And Your Modified AGI Is...	Then You Can Take...
single or **head of household**	$61,000 or less	a full deduction up to the amount of your contribution limit.
	more than $61,000 but less than $71,000	a partial deduction.
	$71,000 or more	no deduction.
married filing jointly or **qualifying widow(er)**	$98,000 or less	a full deduction up to the amount of your contribution limit.
	more than $98,000 but less than $118,000	a partial deduction.
	$118,000 or more	no deduction.
married filing separately	less than $10,000	a partial deduction.
	$10,000 or more	no deduction.
If you file separately and did not live with your spouse at any time during the year, your IRA deduction is determined under the "single" filing status.		

For most people, the requirements for Traditional IRA deductions are easily within reach, and would have a significant impact on FI goals. At his blog, the Mad Fientist shows how contributing to a Traditional IRA instead of a Roth helps save around $100,000 after 20 years!

If you don't qualify for a deduction, Traditional IRAs can still be funded with after tax dollars. The difference from a deductible contribution is that the earnings would also be taxed when withdrawn. It may seem as if this is similar to a taxable account, but tax won't have to be paid on dividends until withdrawn. This works well for tax inefficient investments that pay out dividends or have periodic payments, such as REITs. Non-deductible IRAs can also be used for a technique called the Backdoor Roth, which will be covered in a following section.

Roth IRA

A Roth IRA, while similar to a Traditional IRA, is funded with after tax money, and there aren't any tax deductions that can be made. However, unlike the Traditional IRA, contributions can be taken out at any point, tax and restriction free. A Roth IRA is a great account to invest in before even thinking about a taxable account because of this benefit. Unlike contributions, any earnings must be left in the account until age 59 ½, but a lifetime maximum of $10,000 in earnings can be used tax-free if the money is used to buy a home that you'll live in. Once earnings are taken out, they are completely tax free.

If you want to take tax and penalty-free distributions of earnings, instead of just contributions, two requirements need to be met. First, the IRA must have been initially funded at least 5 years, and second, an allowed reason must exist such as retirement or a disability. The simplest reason is reaching 59 ½ years old, at which point qualified withdrawals of earnings may be made in any amount on any schedule. Becoming disabled or being a "first time" home buyer can provide justification for limited qualified withdrawals.

Some people invest using both a Traditional and Roth IRA to get a limited tax benefit from the Traditional while still being able to access the Roth contributions at any time. It's important to point out that the sum of any contributions to both accounts can't be greater than the total IRA limit for the year. If in 2016, $3,000 is invested into a Traditional IRA, a maximum of $2,500 could be invested in a Roth. These amounts don't count against 401(k) limits, since they are completely separate accounts.

For higher income individuals who don't qualify for the Traditional IRA deduction or for people who are planning on making a big investment in the future, the Roth IRA is an excellent counterpart to a fully funded 401(k). A Roth is also more attractive than a Traditional IRA to people who expect to be in a higher tax bracket when withdrawing money since they would be paying a lower income tax rate in the present than in the future.

Health Savings Account

The Health Savings Account (HSA) is the secret weapon for early retirees and is my favorite account to use because of all the great benefits. A HSA account allows pretax money to be invested and used to cover certain health care expenses with a record of the expense, without having to pay taxes when it is withdrawn! Contributions also reduce taxable income, saving money on income taxes. If there are still funds in the account after reaching age 65, the account can be treated similarly to a Traditional IRA, and any qualifying medical expenses don't need a supporting receipt anymore. Unlike other retirement accounts, FICA taxes for Social Security and Medicare don't need to be paid, essentially giving an automatic return of 7.65% before the money is even invested! All the financial geeks reading this just got weak in the knees, and I hope you've left a cartoon outline in the air because you've just run off to set up an HSA as soon as possible.

What makes the HSA a great account for financial independence is that healthcare expenses can be reimbursed at any time in the future, tax free. This means if you don't immediately need the money to cover any healthcare expenses, the money can be left invested in the account, continue to grow, and eventually be used to cover living expenses during retirement, without paying any taxes. An HSA fund could even be used like a retirement emergency fund, where past expenses would be reimbursed to provide some extra income during tight years.

It might seem that paying for medical expenses with after tax money while there is completely tax free money that could be withdrawn doesn't make sense. This is true when there is a large health care expense like an emergency operation, and using HSA funds would prevent a tight financial situation. In most other cases, where insurance covers most of an expense, the ability to use these funds at any time for when there isn't a steady source of income from a job and unexpected expenses can't be covered as easily. The HSA can also be used to pay for living expenses while executing a technique called a Roth Conversion Ladder, which is covered in a later section.

Most companies also offer matches for HSA contributions, with an average contribution match of $515, which counts toward the yearly contribution limit. Funds from an HSA can be moved from an old employer's account into a new HSA account, but can't be rolled over into a 401(k) or IRA.

To be reimbursed for qualified healthcare expenses, receipts or records for expenses must be submitted to the IRS when filing taxes when withdrawing money from the HSA. If receipts or records are lost, or aren't submitted with tax returns, the withdrawals for those expenses are subject to income tax as well as a 10% penalty.

The only qualification to have an HSA is to be enrolled in a high deductible health plan. The requirement of having a high deductible plan might seem to be a huge negative, but if an emergency fund is used to cover expenses up to the deductible, the HSA and high deductible plan reduces income taxes, while also saving money from the lower insurance premiums.

It is possible set up an HSA at several other providers other than the provider chosen by employers. This is a great benefit because providers vary wildly in their expenses and investing options, so it is worth shopping around for the lowest expenses and funds that match investment goals. If it is not possible to set up automatic payroll deductions with a non-employer provider, FICA taxes will have to be paid, and employer matches might not be paid, so check with your company before making a move to another provider.

To see how an HSA would be used in real life, let's look at how Marco uses his. Marco wants to take advantage of an HSA and decided to switch over to a high deductible health insurance plan, immediately saving him $100 a month on premiums compared to his previous plan. He sets up the HSA through his company's website with Wells Fargo and chooses the funds that the money will be invested in. His plan is to use the HSA for easy access to money during his early retirement years, so he covers any medical expenses with after tax money, while safely filing away the receipts. A few years later, he needs an expensive medical procedure and uses some of the HSA to cover up to his deductible. He submits the receipt for the procedure when filing taxes that year after making sure the procedure was in one of the allowed categories to make sure the withdrawal doesn't get flagged by the IRS. Once he reaches his FI goal amount, he stops working and withdraws funds from the HSA as needed, making sure to submit a supporting receipt for past expenses to match the amounts withdrawn. When he reaches the ripe age of 59 ½, he takes money out at any time and pays ordinary income taxes. Marco still uses it to pay for any medical expenses tax free after he turns 59 ½, now without needing to submit any receipts.

Using an HSA should be a no brainer at this point: it is the only account to avoid **ALL** taxes, and money can be used at any time to cover past expenses, after the money has grown over the years in investments!

Flexible Spending Account

A Flexible Spending Account (FSA) can used to pay for healthcare expenses made during the current year and is funded with pre-tax money. Like other pre-tax contributions, FSA contributions reduce income taxes. If there is a high likelihood of qualifying expenses during the year, it's worth it to set up an FSA. Funds in an FSA can be used to pay for qualifying medical and dental expenses, including copayments and deductibles. Here is a more complete list of generally permitted medical and dental expenses.

A major negative with an FSA is that any funds left in the account at the end of the year are lost. After the Affordable Care Act, some employers allow up to $500 to be carried over into the following year. In some plans, there is a grace period of 2 ½ months after the end of the year to use any remaining funds.

The FSA is most likely the last account anyone should worry about funding because of this use it or lose it catch. Because of this certainty that any remaining funds will be lost, it's better to underfund an FSA than overfund it. If you regularly have physicals and check-ups that aren't covered by insurance, it makes sense to set up an FSA to cover a just those expenses that are almost guaranteed to happen during the year.

Taxable Account

A taxable account is what most people think of when talking about investing, with funds of stocks and bonds being bought and sold through a brokerage. Taxable accounts don't have the tax benefits of 401(k)s, IRAs, or HSAs, but they have much more flexibility and some unique tax strategies that tax advantaged accounts don't have.

Taxable accounts have the widest range of investments to pick from, which you to match investments with your risk tolerance and interests in certain industries or companies. Taxable accounts don't have any restrictions for when money can be taken out, so funds can be bought and sold as needed.

When money is invested in a taxable account, income and FICA taxes are taken from a paycheck, and the investments gains and dividends will be taxed when they are withdrawn. The tax rate for these capital gains depends on how long the investments were held, along with an investor's tax bracket when any gains are realized. Short term gains taxes are paid at the income tax rate on investments held less than a year, and long term gains taxes are for investments held for longer than a year, and are lower than short term gains taxes.

Here is a table from Schwab that shows the long term capital gains rate for each tax bracket as of 2016:

2016 federal income tax brackets

Tax rate on ordinary income	Single		Tax rate on qualified dividends and long term capital gains
	over	to	
10%	$0	$9,275	0%
15%	$9,275	$37,650	0%
25%	$37,650	$91,150	15%
28%	$91,150	$190,150	15%
33%	$190,150	$413,350	15%
35%	$413,350	$415,050	15%
39.60%	$415,050		20%
	Married filing jointly / Qualifying widow or widower		
	over	to	
10%	$0	$18,550	0%
15%	$18,550	$75,300	0%
25%	$75,300	$151,900	15%
28%	$151,900	$231,450	15%
33%	$231,450	$413,350	15%
35%	$413,350	$466,950	15%
39.60%	$466,950		20%

The amount of capital gains taxes can be reduced or completely eliminated for the 10% & 15% tax brackets. In these tax brackets there is a 0% long term capital gains tax, meaning the only time tax is paid is when money is put into the account. This is great for early retirees who don't have a high cost of living and few expenses. Money can be used in retirement practically tax free!

Having money in taxable accounts opens up the opportunity to tax loss and tax gain harvest, which reduces taxes by taking advantage of changes in the price of investments. These techniques can't be used in retirement accounts because any sales and purchases in these funds don't count for taxes. If these methods are unfamiliar, we'll cover them in an upcoming section.

Summing Up the Different Accounts

Hopefully, the past sections have made you start thinking about if you're using the right accounts for your goals, and if there are ways to take greater advantage of the ones you are already using. There are pros and cons to each type of account, and there's not a hard and fast rule for which should be used for your situation. With any kind of financial advice, the ultimate answer to any question is "it depends".

If it doesn't seem clear which accounts would fit your situation, talk with a financial advisor. This book is meant to be a supplement to your financial education, not the definitive and final word on what should or should not be done.

Reducing Taxes & Increasing Contributions

On the journey to financial independence, how much money people make usually isn't the key factor which determines how soon they can retire, but how much they save. The fastest way to save more money is actually to spend less, but how and where that money is then invest also has a huge effect on the time to retirement. The techniques in this section allow investors to save even more money, without having to earn more.

Invest in Tax Advantaged Accounts First

While this book focuses on using every possible strategy there is to get as much money into investments, the single most effective action you can take with the least amount of effort is putting as much money as possible into tax preferred accounts. It's amazing how under-utilized 401(k)s and Traditional IRAs are given how much tax can be avoided. In 2012, only about 17% of Americans even invested using a 401(k), with even fewer investing more than $1,000!

To give an example of the great benefits of these tax advantaged accounts, imagine you had $10,000 to invest from your paycheck. If all of the money was put into a taxable account, you would only be able to invest about $7,500 of the $10,000 after taxes took their portion! Putting all of the money in a pre-tax retirement account will reduce income taxes by $2,500, on top of getting an average employer match of $300. The extra $2,500 can grow tax free. After 40 years, this $2,500 would have grown to almost $40,000 on interest alone! If even more money were contributed to max out the 401(k), along with a Traditional IRA and HSA, the amount of tax avoided would be huge!

Below is a graph from the blog MadFientist.com, where there is a great post on using tax-deferred accounts to retire earlier without investing any additional money. The graph shows two situations where the same amount of money is invested in a tax-deferred account (green bars) or a taxable account (blue line). The red line is the investment goal to retire. It's easy to see from the graph that putting the same amount of money in tax-deferred accounts instead of taxable accounts makes retirement come 2 years!

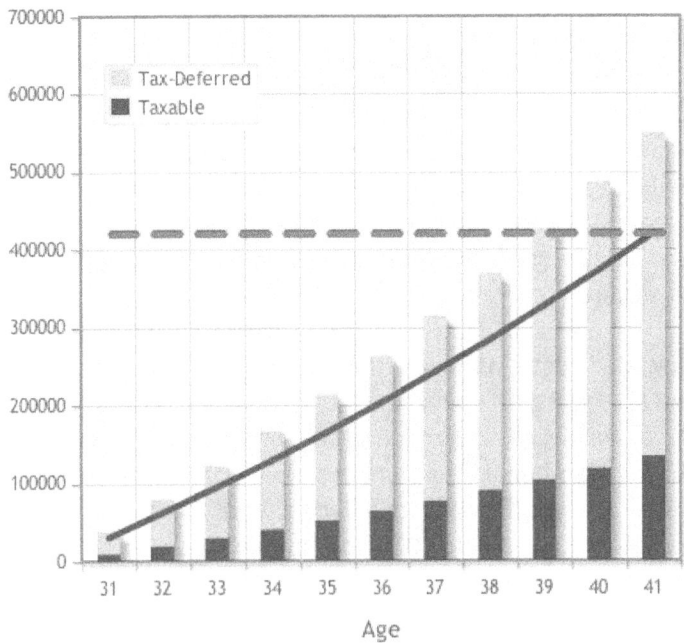

Like most retirees, you will probably be in a lower tax bracket when you use this money, meaning you've avoided a significant portion of taxes when contributing and withdrawing from tax advantaged accounts, all without having to spend any extra money or jump through complex loopholes.

Setting up a 401(k), IRA, or HSA takes about 15 minutes online with a broker such as Vanguard or bank, with many brokers allowing contributions to be set up to automatically invest money from a paycheck or bank account.

The biggest downside to using these tax advantaged accounts is that your money is locked up behind several strict requirements before it can be taken out. When considering the huge tax upside and that this money was always been intended for retirement, it's a great trade off. However, using a Roth Conversion Ladder allows money in these accounts to be accessed before retirement age, so there really isn't a tradeoff between avoiding taxes and using this money.

Backdoor Roth

A Backdoor Roth is a technique for individuals earning more than $132,000 and married couples earning more than $194,000 to contribute to a Roth IRA, an account that would normally be off limits for these high income levels. This technique opens up the opportunity to invest after tax money and withdraw contributions at any time without paying taxes, and withdraw earnings tax free during retirement.

To do a Backdoor Roth, nondeductible contributions are first made into a Traditional IRA, and then converted into to a Roth IRA. The IRS charges a proportional tax on the conversion based on the amount of money that is already in any Traditional IRAs and the amount of converted money. To avoid paying taxes on the conversion, it's best to move any pre-tax funds in Traditional IRAs into a solo 401(k) or employer sponsored 401(k) to avoid the conversion tax.

To see how a Backdoor Roth would be done in practice, suppose we want to get $5,000 into a Roth IRA, but we're above the income limit for a Roth IRA. The money would first be used to buy shares in a Traditional IRA and as soon as the transaction is processed, these shares would be sold and the money would be used to buy funds in a Roth IRA account. This money then can be withdrawn tax free at any time, and any earnings could be taken out tax free after age 59 ½. These contributions would be recorded on forms 1040 and 8606 when filing taxes.

To find out how much of the converted amount will be taxed, the converted amount is divided by the amount of money in any pre-tax IRAs including the contribution and multiply by 100. This gives the percentage of the conversion that is tax free. To get an exact number, the equation is:

$$TF = 100 * [C / (C + B)]$$

C = Amount to Convert to Roth

B = Balances of all pre-tax IRAs

TF = The percentage of conversion amount that is tax-free

Using the numbers from the example above results in:

$$100 * [5,000 / (5,000 + 15,000)] = 25\% \text{ is tax free}$$

If the $15,000 in the Traditional IRA could be transferred into a 401(k), then the formula becomes:

$$100 * [5,000 / (5,000 + 0)] = 100\% \text{ is tax free}$$

After getting past moving money around a few accounts, a Backdoor Roth is fairly straightforward way to contribute to a Roth IRA and being able to access the money very easily. It's a great way for high earners to put money into an account that was previously off limits.

ESPP Plan

An Employee Stock Purchase Plan is a company benefit that lets employees use part of their paycheck to buy the company's stock at a discount or at a previous closing price up to $25,000 a year. An ESPP can be used to create a huge gain even if the stock hasn't grown in value thanks to this discount. If a stock is priced at $100 in the market, and the discounted price is $90, each share can be bought and then sold with an automatic profit of $10! The only catch is contributions are usually made over a length of time set by the company before the stocks are actually bought, so contributions could be made 6 months before any stock is purchased or only a single day beforehand.

As an example of an ESPP in action, the market price of a company stock is $100, with an employee discount of 10%. The holding period is 3 months before shares are bought and sold. $90 is contributed over 3 months and the tax rate will be 25%. We first need to know how long the investment will be tied up. It may seem like it will be 3 months, but only the initial contribution is going to be held for 3 months. The last contribution may only be held for a day. On average, the investment is tied up using the formula a 3 month term divided by 2, or a month and a half. All of the stocks are sold at the end of the holding period for the market price of $100. The $10 spread is taxed at 25%, and resulting in a $7.50 profit. The return is $7.50 divided by 90 days, or 8.33%. 8% is a great return for an investment, especially for such a short period. Well hold on! 8% is not the yearly return. The yearly return is calculated using this formula:

(Ending Value / Beginning Value) ^ (1 / # Years) - 1

This formula gives a yearly return of 89.71%!

If the stocks are sold within a year after being purchased, the IRS taxes any gains at the regular income tax rate, but that doesn't mean the stock should be held longer than a year to avoid higher taxes. In our example above, there is still a significant return, even when including income taxes. Holding the money for at least a year to get a lower tax rate means the market could fluctuation, dropping the price of the stock below its purchase price.

Mega Backdoor Roth

A Mega Backdoor Roth is a technique that supercharges savings into a Roth IRA. It uses several rare features of 401(k)s to contribute up to $34,000 additional dollars to a Roth IRA. These features are in service distributions, which allows money to be taken out of 401(k)s before leaving a company, and after tax contributions (not Roth 401(k) contributions) above the individual 401(k) limit. This allows a work around to the $5,500 IRA limit, meaning even more money can be put into Roth IRA accounts and taken out tax free in the future.

Your 401(k) plan must allow for after-tax contributions beyond the $17,500 limit, preferably up to $52,000 total limit, as well as non-hardship in-service withdrawals of after-tax contributions. When speaking with a representative of either the plan or the brokerage in charge of the plan to find out these details, make sure to make the distinction between Roth 401(k) contributions and contributions above the individual limit. These are fairly rare features of 401(k) plans, so many people can't do a Mega Backdoor Roth.

If your plan doesn't have in-service distributions, it's still possible to do a Mega Backdoor Roth, but you will have to wait until changing jobs to roll the money over to a Roth IRA, where taxes will be paid on the earnings as ordinary income (not long term capital gains).

It's possible to avoid taxes on the earnings, the IRS allows split rollovers which avoids income taxes on the earnings by sending the earnings to a Traditional IRA, and the original contributions to a Roth IRA. This would put off taxes on the earnings until the money is withdrawn from the Traditional IRA. The money that is rolled over into a Roth IRA with an in service distribution will be tax free when withdrawn.

For an example of how to do a Mega Backdoor Roth, we would put $5,000 of after tax money into a 401(k) account (not a Roth 401(k)), and then use an in service distribution to put it immediately into a

Roth IRA. In this example, there weren't any gains to be taxed when converting, so it is fairly straight forward.

The Mega Backdoor Roth is perfect if you're already maxing out pre-tax 401(k) contributions and IRAs and you have extra money to put into a Roth IRA.

Working for yourself

The government loves small businesses. There's so ways to legally avoid taxes and increase the amount of money saved as a small business owner, it's incredible that not everyone is starting their own business right now just for the tax benefits. This section could be a book all by itself, but we'll focus on the biggest impact deductions and techniques available to small business owners.

Global Arbitrage

As a business owner, there are many advantages to being the boss, the largest of which is the ability to decide what to do and the freedom to pursue new ideas. As the boss, anywhere in the world can be your office. Feel like working at a beach? That's your new corporate headquarters for the week. Want to relax at home? Boom, the couch just became a sales desk to make client calls. The ability to work from anywhere opens up a huge opportunity for saving giant wads of cash by living and working in other countries that have cheap costs of living, which is called Geographic Arbitrage.

Arbitrage is when an investor takes advantage of price differences in order to create profit. Geographic arbitrage applies this principal to differences in the cost of living in each country, where money is earned through a job in one country, but spent in a significantly cheaper area. This means you would be able to maintain the same lifestyle at much cheaper price.

To take advantage of geographic arbitrage, it helps to have a job that allows working remotely, rather than commuting to an office every day or having in person meetings as a core requirement. This allows you to earn US dollars, but spend them in a local currency that has cheaper goods. Popular areas to take advantage of global arbitrage are in Eastern Europe, Southeast Asia, Central America and South America, where apartments can go for $200 a month, and a nice meal would be under $5. For a lifestyle that would run $2000+ a month in the US, it would cost around $500-$900 in these areas.

This apartment is on the high end of the price range in Chiang Mai at 12,000 Baht a month, or $336! It comes with a gym, satellite TV, a sauna, and a maid. If you found a place with all of that in the US, it would probably run at least $1,500 a month on the low end.

The first thing you should look at should be the cost of living in a city or country, and if you can maintain the same relative lifestyle. Chiang Mai in Northern Thailand is a popular city for overseas workers and ex-pats, but there are several other cities around the world that offer the same cost savings:

- Kuala Lumpur

- Istanbul

- Panama City

- Bogota

- Buenos Aires

- Cape Town

It's even better if countries also have an exchange rate that is low or declining compared to the US dollar. This means an already cheap country will have all of its prices at a greater discount. The exchange rate shouldn't be the only thing you look for; there are countries with a high difference in exchange rates that also have a high cost of living, so these cancel out and you would end up paying the same or more than in the US.

This would likely be the most drastic change in lifestyle that would also have a huge impact on the amount that can be saved and invested. It would require a change of location, friends, living situation, and possibly even learning a new language, but ultimately, all it would require is booking a flight to another cheaper country and spending your money there. Living abroad isn't for everyone, but there are huge benefits beyond saving money that comes from experiencing new cultures, meeting people that would never have crossed paths with you, and seeing amazing places in our wide world.

Solo 401(k)

For business owners who don't have any employees, a solo 401(k) can be used to put in up to $35,000 additional dollars into a 401(k) account pre-tax. It has the same tax advantaged treatment as a regular 401(k), but has a few features that make it invaluable to FIRE minded entrepreneurs.

1. Up to 20% of self-employed or sole proprietor income can be contributed pre-tax as employee profit sharing, up to the total 401(k) limit of $53,000. This limit includes any employee 401(k) contributions, so if your company 401(k) is already maxed, you would be able to contribute $35,000 more to a solo 401(k) account as a business owner.
2. A solo 401(K) provides the ability to roll over IRAs or old 401(k)s without losing the ability to take advantage of a backdoor Roth IRA.
3. A solo 401(k) gives the ability to invest in funds that are most likely not offered in most employer plans.

The extra contribution space comes from the employer contributions into the plan, which in this case will be you as the employer. The $18,000 personal limit is across all of your 401(k)s, so if you also contribute to a company 401(k) and max out the solo 401(k) first, you won't be able to receive the company match contribution. The ideal order of contributions would be:

1. Contribute the required amount to your main job's 401(k) in order to get the employer match
2. Max out the rest of the personal contribution limit in the solo 401(k)
3. As an employer, contribute up to the $53,000 limit in the solo 401(k)

If you can't set up a business, or are just in the early stages and don't have any revenue, negotiating with your company to contribute part of each paycheck to your 401(k) as employer profit sharing contributions would get the same tax avoidance effect of contributing to a solo 401(k). It's completely possible that a huge amount of taxes could be avoided this way because all invested money could be through personal or company contributions to your 401(k), reducing your taxable income to significantly lower tax brackets. Instead of paying taxes at the 25% bracket, this could lower you down to the 15% or even 10% brackets.

To set up a solo 401(K), all you need is an Employer Identification Number from the IRS. This sounds daunting, but it took me about 10 minutes to fill out a simple form at this IRS website to get one. Once you have an EIN, you can set up a solo 401(k) at a brokerage. The brokerage usually requires a few basic documents to be mailed in or delivered in person to one of the broker's offices that give them the information needed to set up the account.

Once again, the 401(k) leads the pack as the biggest tool to save even more money, with the Solo 401(k) super charging investing ridiculous amounts of money and saving on taxes.

Foreign Earned Income Exclusion

Unfortunately, unlike most countries which only tax income made within their borders, the U.S. counts any income earned anywhere as taxable income. $10,000 made while working in Germany would be taxed the same as $10,000 earned in Florida. However, the IRS gives entrepreneurs working abroad the Foreign Earned Income Exclusion (FEIE), which lets US citizens working abroad to reduce their taxable income by up to $101,300.

One of two conditions need to be met to use the FEIE are:
- **Bona fide resident test**: the taxpayer was a bona fide resident of a foreign country for a period that includes a full U.S. tax year. You do not automatically acquire bona fide resident status just by living in a foreign country or countries for 1 year; the IRS determines bona fide residence from Form 2555, examining the purpose of travel abroad and the length of stay. Because there aren't strict guidelines on this condition, it's hard to determine if a situation will pass the bona fide residence test.

Or
- **Physical presence test**: the taxpayer must be outside the U.S. for 330 days in any 12-month period. The other 26 days spent within the US can be spread throughout that period, and there isn't a minimum amount of time that you have to spend uninterrupted abroad. These 26 days can be spent in the US all at once, or broken up throughout the year. This is the easier and more straight forward of the two conditions to meet.

Taking advantage of the FEIE along with the more lenient tax laws of other countries allows many entrepreneurs to pay no taxes! Many countries don't tax the income of non-residents, though each has a different definition of what a "resident" is, with most defining it as someone who lives in the country for a certain amount of uninterrupted time. Entrepreneurs working abroad will usually have a home base country, and will periodically travel to another country so that they aren't considered a resident and need to pay taxes. Each country has different tax laws and considerations for what a resident is, so if you'd like to go hard core tax avoidance, do some research before buying that plane ticket and flying to Bulgaria on a whim.

This method would effectively remove thousands of dollars of tax burden, something that all the tax advantaged accounts combined couldn't do. Combine this with global arbitrage, and it would save incredible amounts of without a huge amount of effort.

Managing Investments

Once money has been invested, many people don't worry about it anymore, reaping large gains from compounding interest over a long time. However, there are several techniques that improve these investment gains even more by taking advantage of cost differences in investments, and optimizing in which accounts these funds are invested.

Tax Loss Harvesting

Tax loss harvesting (TLH) is when shares that have gone below their original purchase price, or their cost basis, are sold and this tax loss is then used to cancel out any capital gains or reduce taxable income. Up to $3,000 of losses can be used to reduce taxable income each year, and if losses are worth more than $3,000, the extra portion can be used each following year indefinitely until the full loss amount has been used. The money from tax loss harvest sales can be used to buy back into a fund with similar performance, keeping the money growing in the market and prevent missing any market rebounds

Tax loss harvesting may seem like a challenging job to take on alone, and certainly can be if you have a complex portfolio, but for the average investor who has a 401k and a taxable account with different funds in each, it will take no longer than 1 hour to make any sales and fill out tax forms at the end of the year. During the market downturn in January 2016, my Vanguard Explorer fund had a spread of gains and losses, and I decided to take advantage of about $2,000 of losses. I selected the specific shares that I wanted to sell in the fund, leaving out the shares that had gained in value, and sold about $5,000 worth, which had been bought for $7,000. With the $5,000 from the sale, I immediately bought shares of Vanguard's Total Stock Market Index fund. This $2,000 in losses will be counted against my taxable income when I file taxes for 2016, saving me about $500 in taxes. The entire process took 10 minutes of work, or an hourly rate of $3,000. Not too bad of a deal!

To take advantage of a tax loss, all that needs to be done is sell any shares of a fund that have a lower current price than their cost basis. On the next tax return, any realized losses and gains during the year should be recorded on Form 8949 and Schedule D. The short term gains will first be matched with short term losses, with the same occurring for long term gains and losses. The results of these two calculations will be added together to give either a long or short term taxable gain or loss that can be used to reduce your taxable income.

For example, shares of ABC Co. are sold for a $5,000 loss, and there weren't any capital gains to cancel out during the year. $3,000 of this loss would be used to reduce taxable income this year, with $2,000 reducing taxable income on next year's taxes, depleting the loss amount. For another example, if there were also capital gains of $5,000 during the year, the loss and gains would be canceled out, allowing investors to sell shares that have grown in value without paying capital gains taxes.

This tax benefit doesn't completely eliminates taxes, but defers them to a later year, essentially acting as an interest free loan from the IRS. The money that would have gone to taxes can instead be invested and earn even more money. When it comes time to finally pay taxes after avoiding them for several years or even decades, these taxes will be paid with money that is relatively worth less due to the time value of money, where money today is worth more than money in future.

When selling funds, use specific identification to pick only shares that have depreciated in value to sell, rather than a mix of shares with gains and losses. This maximizes the amount of a realized loss instead of selling shares indiscriminately that have gains and losses that would cancel out. Typically, this option will have to be selected for a fund a few days before doing a sale.

It's ideal to reinvest funds from tax loss harvesting sales, so that no market opportunities are missed. Because of the wash sale rule, many experts suggest either putting money into a money market fund and repurchasing the fund or stock after 31 days, or purchasing a fund or stock that has similar performance, but doesn't track the same index. For example, if 100 shares of the Vanguard Total Stock Market Index Fund were sold at a loss, shares of the Vanguard 500 Index Fund, which tracks a different index but has very similar performance, could be purchased and held for 31 days, and then sold to buy back the Total Stock Market Index Fund. If the Vanguard 500 Index fund grows in value, it could be held indefinitely and incorporated into your portfolio. Leaving money in cash or cash equivalents, like a money market fund, isn't ideal, since the money will be sequestered there for 30 days, meaning any market upswings will be missed.

There are a few caveats to watch out for when tax loss harvesting; the most important of which is a wash sale. A wash sale is a rule by the IRS that says substantially similar funds can't be bought 30 days before or after a TLH sale, in any account, not just taxable accounts. This includes 401(k)s, IRAs, or dividend reinvestments back into a fund. If shares were sold in a taxable account, but within 30 days the same fund is bought in a 401(k), this would count as a wash sale. If a wash sale occurs, the loss can't be used to reduce taxes, but will be used to reduce the cost basis of the shares to a lower level. There is no clear ruling by the IRS for what a "substantially similar" fund is, but the intent is to make sure the same fund or stock can't be bought while also getting a tax benefit from the sale of shares of that same fund. The common agreement is that if a fund tracks the same index, it is substantially similar. For example, Vanguard's Total Stock Market Index Fund VTSMX and its ETF version VTI track the same index and are identical in the eyes of the IRS. Other examples would be purchasing stocks of the same company, or buying a Vanguard fund that tracks the same index as a recently sold Fidelity fund. If you are unsure of a potential wash sale, ask a financial advisor for help. A good rule of thumb is if a reasonable person would judge two funds to be substantially similar, then the IRS would as well.

If it still seems daunting to tackle this yourself, there are companies such as Betterment or Wealthfront which will automatically buy and sell funds to maximize taxable events for a fee.

Tax Gain Harvesting

Tax Gain Harvesting (TGH) works on the same principle as tax loss harvesting, but instead of harvesting a loss, shares are sold at a gain to lock in a higher cost basis. It might seem counter-intuitive to want to sell for a gain and pay taxes but harvesting gains can be used with tax loss harvesting to significantly increase the amount of future tax avoidance. It works on the principle of locking in a higher cost basis as share prices rise, which leads to even larger tax loses if shares drop in value. Instead of using the original cost basis when tax loss harvesting, harvesting gains gradually raises the cost basis, meaning losses will that much bigger. Keep in mind there's no change in the money we own when we gain or loss harvest as long as money is kept in the market, it's simply how the IRS tracks investments.

In our tax loss harvesting example, the cost basis was determined when the stock was purchased. If we want to increase the amount we can deduct on taxes as part of a loss, rather than relying on this set tax basis, the cost basis can be gradually increased by selling shares and immediately buying back into the same fund. This updates the cost basis of the shares, and the next time the fund loses value, there will be a larger loss and therefore a larger tax deduction to reduce taxable income over the years.

There is no wash rule for buying back into a fund after realizing a gain, so funds can be bought back immediately, keeping money in the market without missing any market activity. Tax gain harvesting is also great if your expected tax rate in the future is higher than the current tax rate, and taxes are avoided in the future by paying a smaller tax now.

This graph from the Mad Fientist illustrates the difference between just tax loss harvesting and using tax gain and tax loss harvesting together. In this example, assume an investor has bought 1,000 shares at $22 each and that all shares get bought and sold at the same time. In the first scenario, the shares aren't sold and bought as the price increases and when the fund is sold at a loss during the market downturn at the red circle, its cost basis is only $22 per share, resulting in a tax loss of only $4,000.

In the second scenario, tax gain harvesting is used several times to gradually raise the cost basis to $30 per share. This results in a deductible loss of $12,000 when the shares are sold. This is a difference three times larger than the first scenario! This costs $1,200 in long term capital gains, but gives us an additional $2000 in tax savings over the first scenario. This is an $800 dollar difference compared to just tax loss harvesting, even when considering the taxes that were paid along the way.

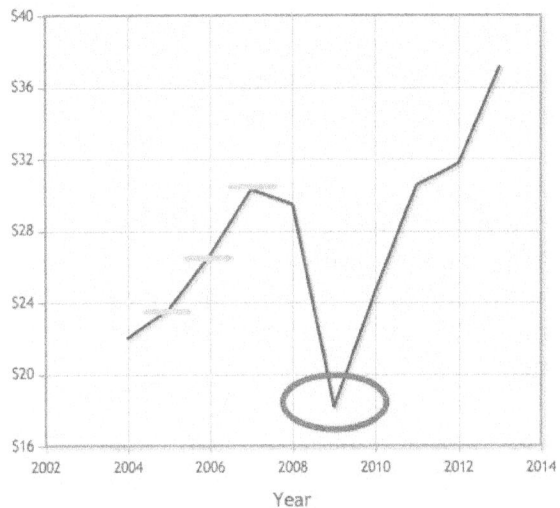

If you are in the 15% tax bracket or below, tax gain harvesting works even more in your favor! As long term capital gains are taxed at 0%, there won't be any taxes paid for harvesting gains, providing a free step up in cost basis to reap an even larger tax loss. However, any shares that have been held for less than a year shouldn't be sold, as there is still short term capital gains tax for every tax bracket.

Tax gain harvesting might seem riskier than loss harvesting if the market is doing very well and continually rising in value. However, the market continually fluctuates, so there will always be opportunities to reap losses to balance out the gains. It's a great method for people in low tax brackets to get an even bigger tax deduction, and still can be an effective method for higher incomes.

Roth Recharacterization

A Roth recharacterization is a method of moving contributions into a Traditional IRA from a Roth IRA, and claiming a Traditional IRA deduction on taxes. This technique is perfect if investors aren't sure if they'll qualify for a Traditional IRA deduction and had been contributing to a Roth IRA. At the end of the year, if it turns out your adjusted income is lower than the Traditional IRA deduction limit, any contributions into Roth IRAs can be moved into a Traditional IRA with a call to the IRA's brokerage, and a deduction can be added to taxes. The IRS treats this money as if it had always been contributed to the Traditional IRA.

My income is above the limit for taking a deduction, so I contribute to a Roth IRA. At the end of 2015, after all of my contributions into 401(k)s and IRAs, my adjusted gross income was actually below the limit, and I recharacterized my contributions from a Roth into a Traditional and took a $5,500 reduction in my taxable income, all for the price of a 15 minute call to Vanguard

If the shares in the fund grew during the year, the growth is taxed as ordinary income, so make sure the tax savings will be greater than this income tax, otherwise it doesn't make sense to recharacterize the contributions. The formula for the tax on these earnings is not very straight forward, so most individuals should work with an accountant to find the tax owed.

To see how a recharacterization would apply to a real life situation, let's look at Robert, who makes $72,000 and is above the limit to receive a tax deduction for Traditional IRA contributions if he has no adjustments to his income. During the year, he maxes out his Roth IRA with $5,500, along with $12,000 contributed to his 401(k). When it comes time to file his taxes, Robert has an adjusted income of $60,000 because of his 401(k) contributions, and finds out he qualifies for a deduction on taxes if he recharacterizes. Before he files his tax forms at the end of the year, he calls Vanguard, and asks them to recharacterize his contributions, and the money is exchanged from his Roth to his Traditional IRA. Since he is in the 25% tax bracket, he saves about $1,375 on income taxes. During the year, the shares grew about $200, so his accountant calculates the earnings that will be taxed and files it as part of his taxes for the year.

Reducing Investment Costs

When picking investments, it's just as important to compare the costs of owning a fund as the potential interest that it could earn. Imagine there were two fairly identical funds. They've had the same performance of about 7% over the last 5 years, and have the same broad diversification across stocks. However, the one point they are different is their expenses. One is passively managed and doesn't have a large marketing budget, while the other is actively managed, has commission loads, and stocks it owns are traded very frequently to rebalance assets. All of this adds up to a larger cost to own the second fund, and results in "Interest Drag". Interest drag decreases how much of a fund's growth will end up in your pocket, changing the second fund's 7% performance into 6% or 5% performance each year! These fees are charged regardless of the fund's performance, which would turn a 2% performance year into a 0% year!

The most common expenses that drag down a fund's performance are:

- Loads - a commission or sales charge that is paid to investment intermediaries (financial planners, brokers, investment advisors) as a sales commission, or is paid as a sales charge when shares are sold.

- 12b-1 fees - These fees are usually around .25% - 1%, and is included in the expense ratio to cover marketing and distribution costs of a fund.

- Fund transaction costs - This is a cost from brokers buying and selling shares either to rebalance risk, move money away from under performing assets, or to incorporate new investments into the fund. These trading costs are included in the fund's operating costs and increase the expense ratio.

- Redemption fees - This expense is meant to discourage early sales of newly purchased shares, and usually applies to sales made within a year of purchase

Another nail in the coffin of these high expense, actively managed funds are that they underperform passively managed funds about 80% of the time, with almost no consistency year to year for which fund or manager will be in the 20% of over performers. This means you'll be paying more to get less returns! To be fair to actively managed funds, they do tend to perform better in market downturns, where managers can move money away from poor investments and into more stable ones. Keep in mind that the market will tend to perform well or average more often then it will underperform, so the stabilization of actively managed funds in market downturns most likely won't outweigh the costs.

Enter the magic of index funds. Warren Buffet famously said "Why look for a needle in the haystack when you can buy the whole haystack?" For everyone who doesn't have the mystical insight of Mr. Buffet, we can still make excellent investing decisions with index funds. Index funds buy groups of stocks that represent a whole market or industry, and are infrequently rebalanced to represent the market. Instead of having to beat the market, funds will perform just as well as the market. Index funds also have the benefit of some of the lowest expenses ratios in the market, leading to less interest drag. A typical actively managed fund expense ratio is around .71%, which doesn't seem like much, but when you have $600,000 invested, this equals $4,440 a year! This is compared to index fund expense ratios of .25% to as low as .06%.

This advice flies in the face of the popular trends in investing and lacks the excitement of having a portfolio manager decide where your money goes. It's definitely exciting to say you have a fund manager giving tips and advice on new investments, but what's even more exciting is making boatloads of money without the help of someone else. Ultimately, the best choice for the average investor, who already works a full time job and wants to maximize possible growth is a passively managed, broadly invested index funds.

Lump Sum Investing

Lump sum investing is where an investor will take their money and, if possible, invest it all at once. This is provides the money more time in the market than more common dollar cost averaging, where investors periodically put equal amounts into investments to even out rising and falling interest rates. This method of investing won't have a huge immediate effect, but over time, as the market grows, it gives about a 4% additional return over dollar cost averaging, which adds up to big fat stacks of money for you.

This is a technique that I use in my 401(k) and IRA accounts to the extreme, where I contribute the maximum allowed amount of each paycheck into my 401(K), and end up hitting the contribution limits about halfway through the year. I'm giving my money as much time as possible to grow into more money, with the added bonus of delaying when a significant portion of taxes are paid.

The advantage to Lump Sum Investing is that your money will have more time in the market, which tends to grow in the long run. Because we want to give our money as much time as possible in the market, Lump Sum Investing should be the preferred investing method if you are given a large sum of money, such as a tax return or year-end bonus at work, instead of gradually using it to buy shares at different prices. This shows the important investing tenet of "time in the market, not timing the market" for retirement investing, where it's almost impossible **to know when is the best time to invest, but it's always good to increase the amount of time your money has to grow.**

Below is a graph from a study done by AB Global, an investment management and research firm, where they compared the historical performance of a fund using dollar cost averaging, lump sum investing, and holding cash.

Display 1
Historically, Investing Immediately Has Maximized Returns

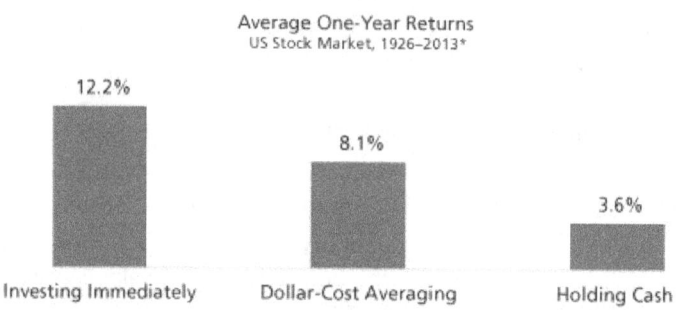

Average One-Year Returns
US Stock Market, 1926–2013*

12.2% — Investing Immediately
8.1% — Dollar-Cost Averaging
3.6% — Holding Cash

Past performance and historical analysis do not guarantee future results.
Historical returns based on 12-month rolling periods from 1926–2013.
"Investing Immediately" is S&P 500 return. "Dollar-Cost Averaging" assumes level investments for 12 consecutive months into the S&P 500 while holding the balance in cash. "Holding Cash" is the three-month Treasury bill return.
Source: FactSet; Roger G. Ibbotson and Rex A. Sinquefield, "Stocks, Bonds, Bills, and Inflation: Year-by-Year Historical Returns," University of Chicago Press Journal of Business (January 1976); Standard & Poor's and AllianceBernstein

They found that when the market is doing well or maintaining its value, which is about 80% of the time, Lump Sum Investing gives a 4% higher average return than Dollar Cost Averaging. In declining markets, Dollar Cost Average works better than Lump Sum Investing, but neither method is as good as holding cash in a bad market. Because the market maintains or rises in value most of the time, Lump Sum Investing will provide a better return than periodic investments most of the time.

Another advantage is that if Lump Sum Investing is used with tax advantaged accounts, taxes will be delayed towards the end of the year. Because of the time value of money, this technique will provide a small savings in the real value of taxes paid on top of the additional possible return.

Rebalancing Funds

Owning investments that match your risk tolerance is an extremely important part of investing. Owning only low risk, low reward assets when riskier but more profitable assets could be bought leads to missing out on greater gains. A portfolio that has disproportionately high risk assets also adds in unwanted risks that outweigh the benefits.

Rebalancing is the practice of buying and selling shares of different assets classes like stocks or bonds in order to bring an investment mix back to the ideal proportions. The desired proportions of classes is called the asset allocation, where the amount owned of each asset class results in a risk/reward trade off. Asset allocations can range from 100% stocks for extremely risk tolerant people to the more moderate 60% stocks / 40% bonds portfolio, all the way to the 100% guns and gold doomsday fanatics. Whatever the allocation is, it is important to periodically readjust assets back to the desired percentages when an asset class has grown or fallen in price.

When rebalancing, there are two options: buying more of an under-represented asset class if the difference from the ideal allocation isn't significant, or selling an over-represented class and buying an under-represented class to quickly bring the allocation back to the desired state. A benefit of rebalancing by selling over performing assets to buy underperforming assets is that the timeless investing advice of "buy low, sell high" is always followed. In the long run, since the market will tend to grow, these underperforming assets will on average grow in value and will have essentially been bought at a discount.

As for how often to rebalance, some people rebalance every time they invest by buying under-represented assets, while others periodically rebalance every 6 months or at the end of the year. Vanguard suggests using 5% thresholds as triggers for rebalancing, where if an allocation goes beyond 5% from its target proportion, funds should be adjusted back to their ideal percentages. Selling over performers does mean there will be added fees and taxes for each trade in taxable account, so less frequent rebalancing is ideal.

For an investor using a lazy portfolio, their ideal asset allocation will be around 60% stocks and 40% bonds. Let's say that in Year 1, their stocks performed poorly and their bonds gained in value, resulting in an allocation of 54% stocks and 46% bonds. Since this is above the 5% threshold, our investor can decide to sell their bonds to buy up more stocks, or they can just buy stocks with new contributions until the allocation is back in line with the desired percentages. In year 2, their stocks rebounded and went to 64% of their portfolio. However, they decide not to take any action, because this is within the 5% threshold they've set for themselves that would trigger a rebalance.

Tax Efficient Investing

Tax efficient investing involves holding certain funds in accounts that also reduce their taxes. An example of this would be holding bonds in a taxable account and stocks that pay out dividends in a 401(k) or IRA, where taxes won't need to be paid on the dividends until they are cashed out. In taxable accounts, it's important to focus on tax efficient funds, such as index funds that don't get bought and sold frequently or have many dividend pay outs.

For example, if there were two index funds, one that paid dividends and gets traded frequently, and one that was very passive, the dividend fund should be held in a 401(K) or IRA where the dividends wouldn't be taxed until the shares are sold, while the second fund would be in held in a taxable account. Another example of tax efficient investing would be owning bonds in taxable accounts, which have a lower expected return and lower tax bill, while holding stocks and higher gain funds in non-taxable accounts.

Beyond the accounts already covered previously, there are other accounts and investments that can be made to focus on tax efficiency. Take these suggestions with a grain of salt as these additional accounts and investments won't fit everyone's financial situation.

1. 529 savings plan
    If you have children or have future higher education needs yourself, it's a good idea to invest money in a 529 plan, which is funded with after tax money. This money is tax free when withdrawn for qualified higher education.

2. US I savings bonds
    I savings bonds are indexed to inflation, and are tax deferred while holding the bond. They can serve multiple purposes in a portfolio (e.g. an emergency fund), and can be used for higher education needs tax-free.

3. Municipal Bonds
    Municipal bonds are a great way to get a steady return, and most of it will be tax deferred. They are loans to cities, states,

or territories that pay out interest over time. The federal government doesn't tax interest from state bonds.

The 529 savings plan is the most straight forward of these three, and owning US I savings bonds and Municipal bonds will add additional tax complications that might not be outweighed by the taxes avoided. It's important to understand the options, but a personal advisor can help figure out which accounts and investments are a good fit for you.

High Interest Emergency Fund Accounts

An emergency fund is an absolute necessity to have for anyone, regardless of their retirement goals. It's a stable fund of money that provides a safety net of funds for, you guessed it, emergencies. Right now, 47% of Americans wouldn't be able to come up with $400 in an emergency! An emergency fund can be used to cover large healthcare costs, unexpected home maintenance, or to cover the cost of living while unemployed. After funding mine, it provided a huge sense of relief knowing that I wouldn't become homeless if I was fired and I could still pay the bills for a few months while looking for another job.

The ideal amount of money in an emergency fund is 3-6 months living expenses, so if each month's living expenses are $2,000, then an emergency fund should have $6,000 to $12,000. This money wouldn't be touched except for emergencies, so many people feel uncomfortable leaving this admittedly large sum of money in a low interest savings account.

This introduces the question of "should emergency funds be invested?" For most people, the answer is a resounding "NO"; an emergency fund isn't meant to provide more money through investing, it's meant to be a guaranteed pool of money to cover worst case scenarios and prevent bankruptcy. The possible interest that could be earned on this money doesn't outweigh the risk that the money can't be accessed quickly or the risk that the money could lose a significant amount of its value, defeating the whole purpose of having an emergency fund.

However, there are ways to earn interest on this money without being exposed to unwanted risk:
1. A high interest savings account

    Most banks offer a checking account that gives less than .1% interest on money, but there are some banks that give 1-6%! The crowd favorite for emergency funds is the Mango Savings Account, which currently gives a 6% interest rate if their requirements of direct depositing money and maintaining a minimum balance are met each month. Another popular account is the Barclays Dream account which offers a 1.05% interest rate. Both of these accounts are insured by the FDIC, meaning the money will always be available even if the banks go bankrupt.

2. Money market funds or I bonds

Money market funds have a slightly higher return than regular bank deposits, and offer some limited growth opportunities, though this is not guaranteed. These accounts are generally stable and don't change in value as much as stocks or bonds. They invest in short term debt like US Treasury bills.

I Bonds are inflation adjusted bonds backed by the US government. They are currently performing at about 1.6% return, giving slightly better performance than a high interest savings account. A sticking point with I bonds is money can't be withdrawn before a year has passed from the purchase date. It's best to purchase them in a ladder fashion so that an older set of bonds can be sold even if newer bonds haven't matured yet.

3. A Tiered Invested Emergency Fund

If you cringe at not investing even a single penny, a strategy to scratch the investing bug with an emergency fund would be to invest tiered amounts in different assets. For example, of the $12,000 needed for the 6 month emergency fund, $6,000 could be kept in a high interest savings account, $4,000 in slightly riskier assets like bonds, and $2,000 could be kept in high risk, high reward assets like stocks. This tiered method at least partially meets the requirement for a stable pool of money that can be easily withdrawn, but also allows for some of the money to be invested.

I use a Mango savings account because it offers the highest interest rate on the market for a saving account. I highly recommend using it for emergency funds, money can be easily moved from the savings account to their checking account online and the requirements to earn the 6% interest are very easy to reach. The account also comes with a debit card that can be loaded with money online and used just like any other card. If you choose to set up an account, and would like to use my referral number (9800045941), Mango will pay me a small referral.

Withdrawing Money Earlier

This is the core of this book. Even after taking advantage of all the tax advantaged accounts and managing them well, it would amount to a whole lot of money that can't be touched until turning 59 ½. The techniques in this section allow this money to be withdrawn regardless of age.

Roth Conversion Ladder

This is by far the mac daddy of FIRE investing hacks. If you read nothing else in the book, pay attention to this section, because it is one of the only ways to access tax advantaged money before reaching retirement age. It allows money that would have been tied up in Traditional IRAs and 401(k)s to be taken out way before retirement age.

This technique works because the IRS lets 401(k) or Traditional IRA funds be converted into a Roth IRA at any time, with income taxes paid on the converted amount. After 5 years, the contributions can be withdrawn tax free from the Roth account. To figure out the amount to convert, many retirees assume that there will be certain inflation rate, and use this to find what their current yearly expenses would be in 5 years if their spending level doesn't change.

During the first 5 years after starting a Roth Conversion Ladder when the first set of conversions have to mature, people use money from taxable accounts or HSAs to live off of until the first conversions can be withdrawn. Some people still work during these years as well, and then officially retire during year 6. Here is a table from the blog Root of Good that shows how conversions and withdrawals could happen for someone who spends about $30,000 a year for living expenses:

	Convert to Roth	Withdraw from Roth	Withdraw from Taxable Account	Age	Notes
2015	$34800	0	30000	45	
2016	35800	0	30900	46	
2017	36900	0	31800	47	
2018	38000	0	32800	48	
2019	39100	0	33800	49	
2020	40300	34800	0	50	5 years since 2015 conversion
2021	41500	35800	0	51	5 years since 2016 conversion
2022	42700	36900	0	52	5 years since 2017 conversion
2023	44000	38000	0	53	5 years since 2018 conversion
2024	45300	39100	0	54	5 years since 2019 conversion
2025	46700	40300	0	55	5 years since 2020 conversion
2026	48100	41500	0	56	5 years since 2021 conversion
2027	49500	42700	0	57	5 years since 2022 conversion
2028	51000	44000	0	58	5 years since 2023 conversion
2029	52500	45300	0	59	5 years since 2024 conversion
2030	54100	46700	0	60	You're over 59.5 – do whatever

For example, assume there is enough money in taxable accounts to live off of for at least the next 5 years. At the start of the first year, you would make a conversion from a 401(k) to a Roth for an amount that is inflation adjusted for expenses 5 years from now. If you live off of $20,000, and inflation is expected to be about 2%, the amount that should be converted is $22,081. Each year, the converted amount gradually rises, so in year 2, the converted amount should be$22,523. At year 6, the original $22,081 could be withdrawn tax free. This can continue until funds in the Traditional IRA or 401(k) have been exhausted or until age 59 ½ is reached and all of the funds can be withdrawn at once.

This technique works particularly well when you have already retired and income is drastically reduced. During retirement, when income from a job is very low or nonexistent, many retirees can fall into the 10% and 15% tax brackets, meaning conversions are incredibly cheap.

While this technique does take a little bit of jumping through hoops, it is also the easiest and lowest risk way to access retirement account money without penalties.

Rule 72t Withdrawals

Rule 72t withdrawals or substantially equal periodic payments (SEPP) are another way to withdraw funds from a Traditional IRA without having to pay the 10% early withdrawal fee. However, it is incredibly risky because if even one payment is messed up and doesn't meet the IRS' withdrawal schedule, all past withdrawals will be subject to the penalty and taxes, no matter how close retirement age is.

Most early retirees should cringe at this using this method since the Roth Conversion Ladder is much easier and doesn't carry the same risk of penalties if you change how much gets withdrawn.

If you do decide to use the SEPP method, the withdrawal schedule is based on average life expectancy, the amounts in the IRA account, and one of three approved calculation methods.

The three methods for calculation the withdrawal schedule are:

1. The <u>Minimum Distribution Method</u> divides the retirement account balance by a divisor from the IRS single or joint life expectancy table. This distribution method results in payments that vary slightly each year, which allows the owner to withdraw the least amount of income possible.

2. The <u>Amortization Method</u> calculates the yearly distribution by amortizing an account's balance over single or joint life expectancy. This results in fixed annual payments that may be best for an individual looking to take out as much as possible from their retirement account.

3. The <u>Annuitization Method</u> uses an annuity factor, which is provided by the Internal Revenue Service, to calculate the substantially equal periodic payments. This method provides a steady, fixed annual payout for the owner.

This chart shows the withdrawal amounts from using each method.

Distribution	Minimum	Amortization	Annuity
Year 1	$2924	$3681	$3699
Year 2	$3148	$3681	$3699
Year 3	$3400	$3681	$3699
Year 4	$3661	$3681	$3699
Year 5	$3940	$3681	$3699
Total	$17073	$18405	$18495

Once started, these withdrawals will have to continue on the same schedule for at least 5 years, even if you are past 59 ½ years old.

It's possible to change the method from annuitization or amortization to the required minimum distribution method only once, so if withdrawals are too small to cover expenses, this will adjust withdrawals to a potentially higher paying method in the long run.

Because of the complications and huge risks with this technique, it's not a preferred method or even that common. If the SEPP technique must be used, it is good to have an accountant to set up withdrawals so they exactly match the schedule.

IRA Horse Race

This is a technique that was popularized by the MadFientist on his blog recently, and supercharges Roth conversions, moving even more money into a Roth without having to pay more taxes. This is built on two main principles: IRA recharacterizations and taking advantage of market fluctuations after converting funds to a Roth.

During the year, investors would convert funds from a Traditional IRA into two Roth IRAs, ideally buying funds in the Roth that move in opposite directions, so that when one fund is up in value, the other fund is usually down. At the end of the year, one of the funds has lost value, while the other fund has gained value. Before filing taxes, the fund that has lost value would be recharacterized back into a Traditional IRA, and taxes won't have to be paid on the first conversion of this money. The end result of this technique is that there is more money in the Roth account than what was converted because of one fund growing, and taxes would only have to be paid on the amount that was left in the Roth.

As an example, at the start of the year, $20,000 is converted from a Traditional IRA and split equally into two separate Roth accounts. One conversion buys a total stock market index fund, and the other buys a total bond market index fund. By the time tax season comes, the stock fund has grown to $15,000, but the bond fund has depreciated to $5,000. The bond fund could be recharacterized back into a Traditional IRA, and taxes would be paid on only the $10,000 that was converted into the total stock market index fund, resulting in $5,000 additional dollars in the fund that aren't taxed.

If both funds appreciate, it might be worth it to keep both funds and pay a higher tax amount. Conversely, if both funds depreciate, both of them can be recharacterized back to a Traditional IRA, and the unused tax space can be used to tax gain harvest if you are still in the 15% tax bracket or lower to take advantage of 0% long term capital gains.

This might seem like it would take a lot of extra work, but it took about 5 minutes and a call to Vanguard for me to recharacterize my Roth IRA contributions, and I will simply need to fill out a form to track it when filing taxes.

Age 55 Rule

Hopefully by this point in the book, 401(k)s are starting to look very attractive. If not, I'm going to add a cherry on top of the 401(k) sundae.

In most cases, you have to wait until age 59 ½ in order to take money out of a 401(k). However, the IRS has given investors a way to get all of the money out a few years early, called the "Age 55 rule". If you leave an employer during or after the year that you turn 55, you can take out all of the money in that company's 401(k), with no extra fees! The money from past company plans is also eligible if it was rolled into the current employer's plan. This rule also applies to all ERISA-qualified, employer-established defined contribution plans, which includes 401(k), 403(b), 501(a) plans, and the federal TSP.

It doesn't matter the reason for leaving the company, it can be from quitting or being fired. Getting another job doesn't cancel out the rule, so quitting Company A after 55 and then getting a job with Company B allows Company A's 401(k) money to be withdrawn. For people who have left their companies before turning age 55 and didn't roll over the 401(k), this distribution method isn't possible.

The age 55 rule doesn't apply to IRA accounts, so any money that was rolled over from a 401(k) to an IRA won't be eligible to be withdrawn without waiting until age 59 ½ or using a Roth conversion ladder.

How It All Ties Together

We've covered a lot of topics and techniques in this book, some of which get very technical very quickly. This section brings it all together and shows how all these techniques can be used to get the most out of your money and retire even earlier without having to earn more.

Enter Robert Lang, our average soon to be early retiree. Robert is 35 years old, has a girlfriend with no kids, and makes $65,000 a year from his job, and an extra $10,000 from his side business. Robert's goal is to save as much money as possible and retire early, so he has cut down on his spending, getting his yearly expenses to $20,000 down from the average cost of living in his city of $25,000.

To show how significant all these steps Robert is going to take for reaching early retirement, we'll compare Robert's results to Rebecca's, who has the same financial situation, but will invest all the money into taxable accounts and not take advantage of any tax advantaged accounts or withdrawal techniques. Because they are both using the 4% rule, their target investment goal is $500,000.

For this example, we'll assume all IRS account limits will remain at the 2016 levels, all numbers won't be adjusted for inflation, and an average investment return of 7% will be used.

Each year, Robert maxes out his 401(k) early in the year using lump sum investing, which reduces his taxable income by $18,000. He also contributes to an HSA and FSA for a total of $3,800, further reducing his taxable income. He also maxes out a Traditional IRA, getting a tax deduction of $5,500 each time he files taxes. In each of these accounts, he invests money into low cost index funds instead of actively managed funds. From his side business, he also establishes a solo 401(k), and contributes $2,000 of the earnings as the plan's employer. He also invests about $23,000 in his taxable accounts. Over the years, he harvests $2,000 on average of losses in his taxable accounts, which are used to further reduce his taxable income. At the end of each year, because of all of the pre-tax contributions he made, he only has to pay taxes on $43,200 of his $75,000 total income. This results in a federal tax of **just $9,071.** Compare this to Rebecca's situation, which is a hefty tax burden of **$17,021**!

After taxes and living expenses, Robert has invested $52,500 each year, whereas Rebecca is only able to invest $38,000. With the amount of money Robert is investing each year, he reaches his $500,000 goal after 7 years, whereas Rebecca reaches it after 10. That's a whole three years that Robert has the financial freedom to do whatever he wants. He can keep working, pursue his hobbies, or volunteers. During these three years, Rebecca has to continue working at a job she's not the most passionate about.

After they both reached their financial goals, Rebecca can use all of her money in her taxable accounts whenever she wants, without jumping through any technical loopholes. However, Robert knows that he can use a Roth conversion ladder to get money out of his tax advantaged accounts just as easily. After starting a Roth conversion ladder, he uses his taxable account, which has grown to about $200,000, to cover living expenses for the first 5 years while conversions aren't available. After five years, he starts withdrawing his first conversion from the Roth IRA, and continues to convert money from his 401(k) and Traditional IRA until both accounts are depleted. He withdraws money from his taxable account as needed to cover any unexpected expenses or large purchases.

Hopefully from this example, you can see the significant impact using these accounts and techniques have on reaching financial independence. For Robert, it had an impact of 3 years; for your situation, it could have an even larger impact.

These techniques are fairly straightforward to use, some can be set on automatic, while others take no longer than an hour to execute each year. A major part of reaching financial independence is cutting back on unnecessary spending and aligning your spending with your long term goals, but what you do with those savings and how you invest them matters just as much.